BEWARE!
KILLER PLANTS

POISONOUS PLANTS

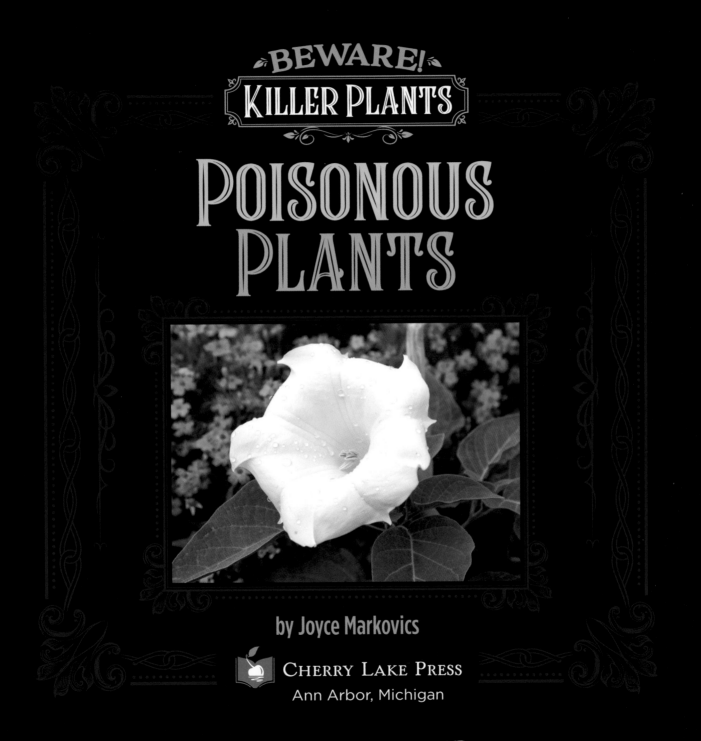

by Joyce Markovics

CHERRY LAKE PRESS
Ann Arbor, Michigan

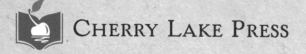

CHERRY LAKE PRESS

Published in the United States of America by Cherry Lake Publishing Group
Ann Arbor, Michigan
www.cherrylakepublishing.com

Reading Adviser: Beth Walker Gambro, MS Ed., Reading Consultant, Yorkville, IL
Content Adviser: Angie Andrade, Senior Horticulturist, Denver Botanic Gardens
Book Designer: Ed Morgan

Photo Credits: © freepik.com, cover and title page; Lincoln Financial Foundation Collection, courtesy of the Indiana State Museum and Historic Sites, 4 top; Public Domain, 4 bottom; Sten Porse, Wikimedia Commons, 5; © emkaplin/Shutterstock, 6; © Veronica Eng/Shutterstock, 7; © Greentellect Studio/Shutterstock, 8; © Tahir Mahmood/Shutterstock, 9; © Steffen Meyer/Shutterstock, 10–11; © Caner Cakir/Shutterstock, 12; © Zuprx51/Shutterstock, 13; © Richard Thornton/Shutterstock, 14; © Sendo Serra/Shutterstock, 15; JNL, Wikimedia Commons, 16; © jessicahyde/Shutterstock, 17; Wikimedia Commons, 18; © Sue J Hill Photography/Shutterstock, 19; © Trambitski/Shutterstock, 20; © Nice_Media_PRODUCTIONS/Shutterstock, 21; © D. Kessler courtesy of Max Planck Institute, 22.

Cherry Lake Press is an imprint of Cherry Lake Publishing Group.

Library of Congress Cataloging-in-Publication Data

Names: Markovics, Joyce L., author.
Title: Poisonous plants / by Joyce Markovics.
Description: Ann Arbor, Michigan : Cherry Lake Publishing, [2021] | Series: Beware! killer plants | Includes bibliographical references and index. | Audience: Grades 4–6
Identifiers: LCCN 2021001259 (print) | LCCN 2021001260 (ebook) | ISBN 9781534187696 (hardcover) | ISBN 9781534189096 (paperback) | ISBN 9781534190498 (pdf) | ISBN 9781534191891 (ebook)
Subjects: LCSH: Poisonous plants—Juvenile literature. | Dangerous plants—Juvenile literature.
Classification: LCC QK100.A1 M377 2021 (print) | LCC QK100.A1 (ebook) | DDC 581.6/59—dc23
LC record available at https://lccn.loc.gov/2021001259
LC ebook record available at https://lccn.loc.gov/2021001260

Printed in the United States of America
Corporate Graphics

CONTENTS

Milk Sickness

The year was 1818 in Indiana. After eating a meal, Nancy Hanks Lincoln felt weak, confused, and sick to her stomach. Seven days later, the 34-year-old mother was dead. She left behind a young son named Abraham, who would grow up to be one of America's greatest presidents.

A portrait of Nancy Hanks Lincoln

President Abraham Lincoln

White snakeroot

Young Abe was crushed by the loss of his mother. At the time, no one knew that a plant—called white snakeroot—had poisoned Nancy.

WARNING: Plants can be deadly. Never touch or eat an unfamiliar plant.

White snakeroot grows in fields and woods across North America. The plant has many stems and clusters of white flowers. It's also tall—about the same height as a fourth grader. Every part of the plant contains a killer toxin called tremetol.

The flowers of the white snakeroot

Cows often graze on snakeroot. When they eat a lot of the plant, the toxin can make them sick. And their milk and meat can become poisonous. People who consume milk or meat from the cow may become sick with deadly "milk sickness."

White snakeroot can sicken and kill cows, horses, and other animals. Before they die, they stagger around and then collapse.

During the 1800s, thousands of people died from milk sickness. White snakeroot was finally identified as the cause of the illness in the 1920s.

A Poisonous Garden

White snakeroot is one of hundreds of poisonous plants. These deadly plants come in many shapes and sizes. Some, like oleander, have attractive flowers. But one bite of an oleander's bloom, leaf, or branch can kill an adult.

Yellow oleander is also toxic. Honey made from oleander flowers can be poisonous.

Campers are said to have died after grilling meat using oleander branches as skewers. Even smoke from burning oleander is poisonous. Oleander contains oleandrin. This toxin causes stomach upset and weakness, and it can stop the heart.

In 2000, two young children died in California after chewing on oleander leaves.

Another poisonous plant with stunning flowers is aconite, or monkshood. Because of its deadliness, it's known as the queen of poisons. People often mistake monkshood roots for edible horseradish roots. In 1856 in Scotland, a cook killed two priests after accidentally grating monkshood root into a sauce.

Experts believe most plants use poison for protection against hungry animals.

All parts of monkshood are dangerous. Simply touching the plant can result in poisoning. The poison is so potent that scientists once thought about using it to make deadlier bullets.

Monkshood grows across Europe and North America. Here it's shown growing in Austria.

A vine called rosary pea might have the world's deadliest seeds. The plant winds around trees in Africa and Asia. It can climb up to 15 feet (4.6 meters). After flowering, a rosary pea produces red-and-black seeds that look like ladybugs.

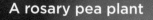
A rosary pea plant

Abrin is the name of the rosary pea's poison. Abrin breaks down and kills cells in the body. After a few hours or days, a victim will experience nausea, convulsions, organ failure, and death. Eating just one seed can "kiss a child to death," said a doctor.

The killer seeds of the rosary pea

People sometimes use rosary pea seeds to make jewelry. There are tales of jewelry makers dying after doing so!

The datura has trumpet-shaped white or purple flowers. It grows worldwide.

DEADLY DATURA

Jimsonweed, or datura, is another well-known killer. In the fall, the plant produces a creepy-looking, spiky seedpod. Inside the pod are dark brown seeds. In 1983, a Canadian woman collected the seeds. Mistaking them for spices, she mixed them into a hamburger patty and ate it.

Half an hour later, the woman was delirious, and her heart was pounding. Soon, she was fighting for her life. She spent 24 hours in a coma. After 3 days, she was released from the hospital. The woman was lucky to survive her brush with the deadly datura.

All parts of the datura are toxic, especially the seedpods and seeds.

Datura poisoning has also been linked to **zombies**. In Haiti, an island country in the Caribbean, zombies are believed to exist. After traveling to Haiti, scientist Wade Davis learned that so-called zombies are really living people who may have been drugged with datura.

Datura, or zombie cucumber as it's called in Haiti, can put people into a deathlike state. If people are given a small amount each day, it's possible they could survive. But they might walk around in a zombie-like trance!

The fruit of the datura, or zombie cucumber

An 1887 illustration of a belladonna plant

Datura is part of the nightshade family of plants. This family includes vegetables such as potatoes, eggplant, and peppers. However, the family includes several known killers. Another is the deadly nightshade, or belladonna.

Belladonna grows in North America, Europe, and Asia. In the fall, the plant produces shiny black berries. The berries look tasty to some, especially children. In 1880, a Virginia farmer's three children died after eating belladonna berries. The man never forgot the plant that killed his family.

Just two deadly berries from the belladonna plant can kill a child.

Belladonna means "beautiful woman" in Italian. Long ago, women put the juice of the berries in their eyes to make them appear larger.

Poison Hemlock

In Scotland, a common poisonous plant is called dead man's oatmeal—and for good reason. In 1845, a Scottish tailor bit into a sandwich his children had made for him. It contained parsley they found in the garden—only it wasn't parsley. It was poison hemlock, a relative of parsley. In a matter of hours, the man was dead.

Poison hemlock has a smooth green stem that can be streaked with purple or red.

The most famous person to die from poison hemlock was the Greek philosopher Socrates. After swallowing the poison, numbness crept through his body. The poison took several hours to reach—and stop—his heart.

Socrates died in 399 BCE—more than 2,000 years ago!

Poison hemlock is part of a family that includes carrots. It was first grown in Europe and North Africa but is now found in many other parts of the world.

PLANT PARTNERS

Plants and animals sometimes help one another.
This type of relationship is called mutualism.

Datura flowers open at night. Their sweet smell attracts nocturnal hawk moths. These large moths hover above the flowers like hummingbirds. Then they insert their long mouthparts deep into the flower to suck its nectar. In return for the sweet treat, the moths pollinate the flowers.

Datura
The sweet-smelling flowers open at night when hawk moths are active.

Hawk Moth
While hawk moths suck the datura flowers' nectar, they pollinate the flowers. This helps the plant reproduce.

GLOSSARY

coma (KOH-muh) a state in which a person is unconscious and cannot wake up; can be caused by toxins

consume (kuhn-SOOM) to eat or drink

convulsions (kuhn-VUHL-shuhns) sudden, uncontrollable, jerky movements

delirious (di-LEER-ee-uhss) a state of mental confusion in which one may see or hear things that are not real

nausea (NAW-zhuh) a sick feeling in one's stomach

nectar (NEK-tur) a sweet liquid produced by plants

nocturnal (nok-TUR-nuhl) active at night

philosopher (fuh-LOSS-uh-fur) a person who thinks and writes about life

poisoned (POI-zuhnd) harmed or killed by a chemical or other substance

pollinate (POL-uh-nayt) to carry pollen from one flower to another, which fertilizes the second flower, allowing it to make seeds

potent (POH-tent) powerful or strong

priests (PREESTS) people who perform religious ceremonies

relative (REL-uh-tiv) something that's connected or related to something else

toxin (TOK-sin) a poison produced by certain plants or animals that can cause sickness or death

victim (VIK-tuhm) a person who is hurt or killed by something

zombies (ZOM-beez) people in a trancelike state who are believed to have died and been brought back to life

23

Find Out More

Books

Lawler, Janet. *Scary Plants*. New York: Penguin Young Readers, 2017.

Miller, Connie Colwell. *The Deadliest Plants on Earth*. Mankato, MN: Capstone Press, 2010.

Thorogood, Chris. *Perfectly Peculiar Plants*. Lake Forest, CA: Words & Pictures, 2018.

Websites

The Alnwick Garden: The Poison Garden
   https://www.alnwickgarden.com/the-garden/poison-garden/

Brooklyn Botanic Garden: Jimson Weed
   https://www.bbg.org/news/weed_of_the_month_jimson_weed

National Capital Poison Center: Poisonous and Non-poisonous Plants
   https://www.poison.org/articles/plant#poisonousplants

Index

About The Author

Joyce Markovics enjoys writing about and collecting unusual plants. One of her favorites is a feathery plumosa fern, which isn't a fern at all. It's actually part of the asparagus family of plants.